ZEITUNG

Mit Wörterbuch und Vokabelhilfe

Manfred Mai

Englisch lernen mit den Leselöwen

Detektivgeschichten

Aus dem Deutschen übersetzt von David Ingram

Zeichnungen von Wilfried Gebhard

Loewe

Bibliografische Information Der Deutschen Bibliothek
Die Deutsche Bibliothek verzeichnet diese Publikation in der Deutschen Nationalbibliografie; detaillierte bibliografische Daten sind im Internet über *http://dnb.ddb.de* abrufbar.

Der Umwelt zuliebe ist dieses Buch auf chlorfrei gebleichtem Papier gedruckt.

ISBN 3-7855-5332-3 – 1. Auflage 2005

Die deutsche Originalausgabe erschien 1998 im Loewe Verlag unter dem Titel „Leselöwen-Detektivgeschichten"
Aus dem Deutschen übersetzt von David Ingram
Umschlagillustration: Wilfried Gebhard
Umschlaggestaltung: Andreas Henze

www.loewe-verlag.de

Contents

Liebe Eltern,

unaufhaltsam hält die englische Sprache Einzug in den kindlichen Wortschatz. Was die Sprachwissenschaft nüchtern als Anglizismen betitelt, finden die Kinder überaus spannend. Mit ungebremstem Wissensdurst machen sie sich daran, erste Worte oder Sätze in einer Fremdsprache zu erlernen und zu kommunizieren.

Kinder sind relativ früh mit dem Englischen vertraut, spätestens seit der Einführung des Englischunterrichts an den Grundschulen. Eine Fremdsprache spielerisch, ohne Erfolgszwang, dafür aber mit schnellen Erfolgserlebnissen lernen, so lautet das Motto.
Dieses Prinzip haben wir auch den Englisch-Ausgaben unserer Erstlese-Reihe *Leselöwen* zu Grunde gelegt. In abgeschlossenen Geschichten können die kindlichen Leser ihre ersten Englischkenntnisse anwenden und vertiefen. Die Sprache ist einfach gehalten, die wichtigsten Vokabeln sind im Text markiert und werden in ihrer konkreten Bedeutung am Rand auf Deutsch erklärt. Verben werden dabei gleich in der jeweiligen Person, Adjektive in der flektierten

Form übersetzt. Der Sinn eines Satzes lässt sich so schnell und ohne lästiges Nachschlagen erschließen. Viele Begriffe werden zusätzlich in den Illustrationen durch Wort-Bildzuweisungen erläutert.
Im Anhang finden sich sowohl die wichtigsten Vokabeln aus dem Text in alphabetischer Reihenfolge als auch ein speziell dem jeweiligen Thema zu Grunde gelegter Wortschatz auf einer praktischen Ausklappseite.
Die Verben stehen hier im Infinitiv, da an dieser Stelle der Hauptakzent eher auf der Erweiterung des Wortschatzes als auf der Erschließung eines Wortes innerhalb eines Satzes liegt. Dabei werden nicht alle möglichen Bedeutungen im Deutschen angegeben, sondern nur die wichtigsten.
Und wenn Sie mit Ihrem Kind gleichzeitig auch das Hörverständnis und die Sprechfertigkeit trainieren möchten, sind bei Jumbo zu jedem englischen *Leselöwen*-Band die entsprechenden Hörkassetten erhältlich.

Viel Spaß und Erfolg mit
„Englisch lernen mit den Leselöwen"
wünscht Ihnen Ihr

Leselöwen-Englisch-Team

36
30
8

Brilliant detectives

Axel sits alone in front of the television, watching "Sherlock Holmes".

When the brilliant detective sets a trap for the thief, Axel's sister Antonia comes into the room. "Hey, Axel! At the swimming pool today, somebody stole money and clothes from four lockers. The police don't know who did it."

Axel looks at his sister. "A thief breaks into four lockers, and nobody notices?"

sets a trap: eine Falle stellt
stole: stahl
lockers: Schließfächern
breaks into: bricht ein
notices: bemerkt

"That's the strange thing. There are no marks on the lockers at all. But now the lockers are empty." Antonia grins. "It sounds like a job for you, Mister Brilliant Detective."

Axel doesn't answer. He goes to the phone, calls his friend Kevin, and describes the case to him.

strange – *sonderbare*
no marks … at all – *überhaupt keine Spuren*
grins – *grinst*
describes the case – *schildert den Fall*

"See you at the swimming pool!" Axel says.

Ten minutes later they meet at the pool.

They go to the lockers and have a look at them. There are no marks on the outside.

"The thief had keys to the lockers," Axel says.

"Stolen keys, I bet," Kevin says.

Axel shakes his head. "No, I don't think so," he answers. "Because the locker owners still have their keys."

Kevin understands what Axel means. "So the thief found the keys somewhere else?"

Axel starts to think hard. "The people here had keys. The thief had keys, too. But where from?"

Schließfächern

keine Spuren

Schlüssel

Gestohlene; wette

Schließfach-besitzer

meint

hatten

woher

Suddenly Kevin has an idea. "Perhaps the pool attendant has a second pair of keys!"

"Hmm," Axel says. "Perhaps. Then he is a suspect."

"We must tell the police," Kevin says.

"No, wait," Axel replies. He tries to take the key out of the lock, but it is stuck.

"Have you got a coin?"

Kevin gives him one. "I want it back, though."

Axel puts the coin in the slot and turns the key. The key comes out.

"And now?" Kevin asks.

Axel looks at the key in his hand. "I think I've got it," he says. "It's easy to take a key away from here. And there's a man in the supermarket who makes copies of keys.

Plötzlich
Bademeister
Schlüssel
Verdächtiger
antwortet
steckt fest
aber
(Geld)Schlitz
dreht … herum

So all a thief needs to do is bring the right key back again later, and then he can steal things any time he wants!"

"Very clever," Kevin says, and takes his coin back out of the locker.

"So either the thief has a copy of the key, or it was the swimming pool attendant," Axel says. "Now we must wait and see who opens more than one locker."

tun muss
Schlüssel
stehlen
Schließfach
entweder
oder
Bademeister

The boys pretend to sunbathe, and keep a very close eye on the lockers at the same time. Half an hour later they see a young man with a big bag. He opens a locker, looks inside it, and shuts it again. Then he opens another locker!

"That's him!" Axel whispers. "Get the pool attendant – quickly!"

The young man takes something from the locker. Then he goes to another one.

pretend to sunbathe: tun so, als würden sie sich sonnen
keep a very close eye: behalten genau im Auge
lockers: Schließfächer
whispers: flüstert
pool attendant: Bademeister

Axel is very nervous. He looks for the pool attendant.

Then Kevin comes back with the attendant and a helper.

"That's him!" Axel shouts and points at the thief.

"Hey, you! What do you think you're doing?" the attendant shouts.

The thief spins round very quickly and starts to run away.

Bademeister

Was machen Sie da?

dreht sich um

lockers

Too late! The swimming pool attendant and his helper block the way.

"I … I want to get my things out of my locker," the thief says. It is a lie.

"He's got a copy of the key," Axel says.

"Let me see that key," the attendant says.

Suddenly the thief runs off, but the attendant and his helper catch him.

The attendant calls the police. They arrive shortly afterwards. Axel and Kevin tell them how they found out about the thief.

The policemen are very impressed. "You boys are brilliant! You could teach Sherlock Holmes a thing or two!"

Bademeister
versperren
Schließfach
Lüge
Schlüssel
Plötzlich
danach
herausfanden
beeindruckt
beibringen

Who was it?

One evening, Lena is doing her homework. She puts her pen down and has a stretch. Then she gets up, goes into the kitchen and opens the fridge.

streckt sich

Kühlschrank

"Where is it?" she murmurs. She moves the butter and a jam jar to one side. "I don't believe it," she says, and calls out: "Why is my yoghurt not here?"

murmelt

"I don't know," Florian says from the living room.

Lena opens the door.

"Nor do I," Stefanie says. "I'm too small to open the fridge by myself."

"Liars!" Lena says angrily. "You always steal my yoghurt and then deny it!"

"I don't like strawberry yoghurt anyway," Florian says.

Lena decides to go to Philipp's room.

"Where is my yoghurt?" she asks him.

"I don't know," Philipp answers. "Now get out of my room!"

"I want to know where my yoghurt is!" Lena says.

"Go away!" Philipp answers. He picks up a book and tries to throw it at her.

Ich auch nicht

Lügner

stehlt

leugnet

sowieso

beschließt

Lena slams the door and goes into her room. "Just you wait till I find out," she murmurs. She lies on her bed and wonders how to catch the thief. Then she suddenly snaps her fingers and grins.

"That's it!" She gets up, puts on her shoes, goes to the supermarket and buys a strawberry yoghurt.

schlägt ... zu
Warte du nur
fragt sich
plötzlich
schnipst; grinst

Back home she opens the carton, eats half of it, and puts the rest on a plate. Then she puts ketchup, mustard, flour and pepper into the carton, and stirs it all up. The mixture is too red, so Lena adds two more spoons of flour. Then she puts a little bit of yoghurt on top, to hide everything.

Jogurtbecher

Senf

Mehl; Pfeffer

rührt alles um

Gemisch

fügt hinzu; Löffel

obendrauf; verstecken

She puts the lid back on, and puts the carton into the fridge. Then she goes back to her room and leaves the door open slightly, so that she can hear what happens.

Lena is nearly asleep when she suddenly hears somebody downstairs shouting “Yuk!” She jumps out of her bed, rushes down the stairs and into the kitchen. She sees her father in front of the kitchen sink, spitting out Lena’s special yoghurt.

“So it was you!” Lena says in surprise.

Her father coughs.

Lena’s mother comes in from the living room. “What’s going on here?” she asks.

“Daddy ate my favourite yoghurt and …”

Deckel
Kühlschrank
lässt
etwas offen
schläft
plötzlich
rennt
Küchenspüle; spuckt aus
überrascht
hustet
aß

Lena's father interrupts her. "Favourite yoghurt? It's disgusting! Which shop is it from?"

fällt ins Wort

ekelhaft

Now Philipp, Stefanie and Florian all come down to the kitchen.

"What's all this noise?" Philipp asks. "We can't sleep."

"Daddy ate something bad," their mother explains.

"Something bad!" the father says, and he holds the carton under his wife's nose. "It's absolutely revolting!"

Lärm

aß

erklärt

vollkommen widerlich

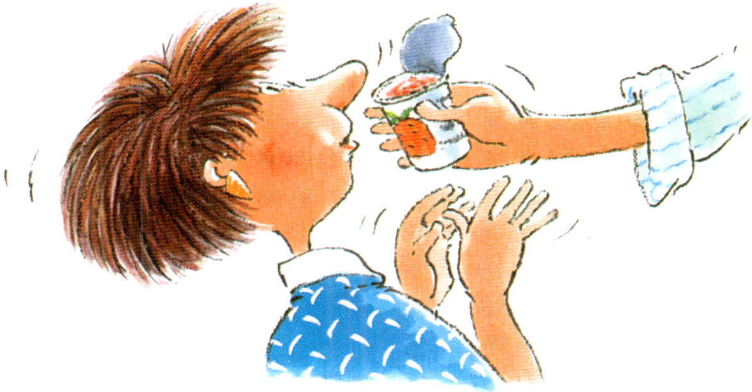

Their mother sniffs at the carton. "It smells a bit like ketchup," she says.

"It was me," Lena says.

riecht

Then Lena tells them the whole story. She says to her father: “Now I know that you always eat my favourite yoghurt.”

Her mother grins. Her father shakes his head, but then he smiles. “You are a very clever girl,” he says. “When you are older, you must become a detective.”

whole: *ganze*
grins: *grinst*
become: *werden*

The ring thief

It is Mummy's birthday. The Koller family drives to a restaurant for lunch.

Nine-year-old Saskia likes restaurants, but her sixteen-year-old brother Stefan does not. He decides to come along anyway, because it's Mummy's birthday.

trotzdem mitzukommen

The restaurant is very full. The Koller family sit down at the last free table. A waitress comes over.

Kellnerin

Saskia has to go to the loo. Her Mummy goes with her, to wash her hands. When they come back the drinks are already on the table.

Daddy raises his glass and says: "Happy Birthday, Mummy." So do the children.

The family waits for the food. Daddy starts to build a house of cards with the beer mats. Mummy watches him, and Stefan looks at the other people in the restaurant.

Klo

erhebt

Bierdeckeln

"My ring!" Mummy says suddenly. "I left it on the basin!" She gets up quickly and goes to the toilet. Then she comes back again.

plötzlich

Waschbecken

She shakes her head. "It's not there any more." She is very sad.

"The new ring that Daddy gave you for your birthday?" Saskia asks.

Her mother nods. "Yes. It's real silver, and worth a lot."

"One of those three women has it," Stefan murmurs.

"I beg your pardon?" his father asks.

"The blond lady there, the bunette by the door, and the

not … any more: nicht mehr
nods: nickt
real: echt; worth a lot: viel wert
murmurs: murmelt
I beg your pardon: Wie bitte

redhead with the white blouse by the window. They all went to the loo after Mummy did."

"You can't just say that they are thieves!" his father says.

"Yes I can," Stefan says.

He gets up and goes over to the blond lady.

"My name is Stefan Koller.
I am a private detective
and I have
a question."

The woman looks at Stefan in surprise.

"Did you see a ring on the sink in the toilet?"

"Er … there was a ring there, yes."

"Well?" Stefan asks.

"Well what?"

"What did you do with the ring?"

"Nothing."

Rothaarige

Klo

überrascht

Waschbecken

"You did nothing?"

The woman nods. "That's right. I hope you don't think I'm a thief?!"

nickt

hoffe

"I don't think anything," Stefan answers. Thank you for the information." Now he goes to the brunette lady, and asks her the same question.

"I never saw a ring," answers the lady.

"Go away little boy, and leave my wife alone!" her husband says.

lass … in Ruhe

Ehemann

Stefan goes over to the lady by the window.

"A private detective?" she asks. "Aren't you a little bit too young?"

"I have a question for you," Stefan answers. "When you went to the toilet just now, did you see a ring on the basin?"

Waschbecken

"A ring?" the woman asks.

Stefan nods. "Yes."

nickt

The woman shows Stefan both her hands.

"No. As you can see, I have a ring on every finger. A silver ring would not suit all these. And now would you please go away and leave me in peace?"

würde nicht passen

mich in Ruhe lassen

"Thank you for the information," Stefan says, and he goes back to his family.

"The people are surprised, Stefan," his mother whispers. She is embarrassed. "Sit down again."

überrascht

verlegen

"Don't worry, Mummy," Stefan answers. "I know which woman stole your ring now."

"You're quite certain?" his father asks.

"Absolutely certain," Stefan answers. "And now I must phone the police."

Stefan goes over to the telephone, and calls the police.

Mach dir keine Sorgen

welche; stahl

Bist du ganz sicher?

Absolut

Clever Carola

Hey!

Hey, you!

Yes, you!

You don't need to look round, you can't see me.

May I introduce myself? My name is Clever Carola. I'm a detective.

Darf ich mich vorstellen?

What? You've never heard of me? I don't believe it!

Du hast noch nie gehört

Anyway, let me tell you about my last case.

letzten Fall

One day I'm in my deckchair outside the house. I hear someone in the street shout: "Damn! It must be here somewhere!"

It is Sabine's voice. Sabine is a real pest.

Every day she loses something at least ten times and then I have to find it again. I'm an important detective and I need my rest. So I go back to sleep.

But pests like Sabine don't care about that.

"Hey, Carola! Can you help me look?"

Help me look? Huh! Silly girl! A great detective like me doesn't look, a detective investigates. That's something Sabine doesn't understand at all.

Liegestuhl

Stimme

Nervensäge

verliert

mindestens zehnmal

Ruhe

ermittelt

"Carola, wake up!" Sabine tugs at my sleeve.

"What's the matter?" I ask her, sleepily.

"I've lost the key to my flat," Sabine answers.

I look at my watch. If I have a case to solve, I want to know how long I need to solve it.

"Where?"

"What do you mean, where?" Sabine asks.

"Where did you lose it?"

zerrt; Ärmel
Was ist (denn) los?
verschlafen
Schlüssel
Fall; lösen

"How do I know? I've lost it!" — *Ich habe ihn verloren*

Today Sabine is right, for a change. — *zur Abwechslung*

"Sorry," I tell her, "but I don't have any time."

Sabine takes a bag of jelly babies out of her pocket. "If you find it you can have half of these." — *Gummibärchen*

Sabine knows what I like.

"All right, I accept the case. But I want ten jelly babies in advance." — *nehme an; Fall* — *im Voraus*

Sabine agrees. — *ist einverstanden*

"Okay, first question. Is there a spare key?" — *Ersatzschlüssel*

Sabine nods. — *nickt*

"Then use that instead," I suggest. — *stattdessen* — *schlage vor*

"I haven't got it. It's hanging in the flat."

"How stupid can you get?" I ask, shaking my head.

"Okay, second question: does anyone else have a key to the flat?"

Schlüssel

"Yes. My Mummy does, of course."

"So why don't you get it from her?" I ask.

"Because Mummy is at the office," Sabine answers. "And I have to be home before her to make the supper."

Büro

"Third question: when did you last have the key?"

Sabine thinks about this.
"When I went out of the flat to buy bread, I think."

"Did you lock the door?"

Sabine shrugs her shoulders.

"Think hard!" I tell her, and eat a yellow jelly baby.

Hast du abgeschlossen

zuckt mit den Schultern

Sabine frowns. "No, I didn't lock the door. I only closed it."

"Aha!"

"Why is that so important?" asks Sabine.

"I'm the one who asks the questions here. Okay, question four: where do you put the key when you leave the flat?"

"I hang it round my neck." Sabine looks down. "But it's not there now."

When she lifts her head again, I see something. "Turn round!" I tell her.

"Why?"

"No questions! Just do what I say!"

"You lie here on the deckchair, eat my jelly babies and talk nonsense," Sabine says. "Help me look!"

frowns: runzelt die Stirn
neck: Hals
deckchair: Liegestuhl; jelly babies: Gummibärchen
nonsense: dummes Zeug

I eat the rest of the jelly babies. "If you turn round, I can tell you where the key is."

"Don't be silly," Sabine says.

"There it is," I say proudly.

"Where?" Sabine asks.

"Right behind you," I answer. "Not on the ground! On your back!"

It takes a while before Sabine understands. Then she is very relieved.

Gummibärchen

Schlüssel

stolz

Boden

Rücken

erleichtert

Clever Carola, the great detective, has solved another case yet!

In exactly four and a half minutes. And without having to leave her deckchair even once. I bet nobody else can do that!

So if you have a problem and need help, just ask for Clever Carola.

Hey! You!

Yes, you!

Did you hear what I said?

Good!

hat ... gelöst

Liegestuhl; auch nur einmal; wette

A mysterious man

Vanessa and Marvin are on holiday with their parents in a hotel in the Bavarian Alps. Mummy and Daddy want to do something healthy. They jog, they climb the mountains, they lift heavy weights, they have massages and they go to the sauna and the whirlpool. Vanessa and Marvin really like the whirlpool.

Gesundes

Massagen

Soon Vanessa and Marvin get bored. They don't like all the sport, and they prefer to stay in the hotel. Then they suddenly notice a man who behaves very strangely. Before he leaves his room, he sticks out his head and looks all around. Then he crosses the corridor, but doesn't use the lift. Instead, he takes the stairs. Then he goes out of the back door to the car park, throws something inside a car, and goes back into the hotel.

"He's very suspicious," Vanessa says.

"I think he's a thief," Marvin says.

The two children decide to find out more about the mysterious man.

langweilen sich

ziehen es vor

plötzlich; bemerken

sich sonderbar benimmt

steckt heraus

überquert

Aufzug; stattdessen

verdächtig

beschließen

geheimnisvollen

Vanessa and Marvin watch the man's door closely. Nothing happens – but then the door suddenly opens, and the man's head appears. He slips out of the hotel again, just like a thief.

"He's a robber!" Marvin whispers.

"Quick, let's follow him!" Vanessa says.

The man goes to the car again. He looks round, and takes off his dressing-gown.

genau
plötzlich
erscheint
schleicht heraus
Räuber
Morgenrock

Then he throws it into the car and walks off. The children notice how fat the man is. The man jogs into a forest. The children follow him. The man starts to puff and blow like a walrus. Soon, he is so exhausted that he sits down on a bench.

bemerken

schnaufen; keuchen

Walross

erschöpft

Bank

He rests on the bench for a while, and then starts to jog again. Then he goes back to the car park, puts his dressing-gown back on and quickly goes back to his room.

"That's strange," Vanessa says. "He didn't do anything suspicious. Perhaps he isn't a thief at all."

"Then why does he act so suspiciously?" Marvin asks.

Vanessa shrugs her shoulders.

The next day the man slips out of his room and goes down to the sauna. He looks through the little window – nobody is inside. Then he goes over to the gym, listens at the door, and goes inside.

rests: ruht sich aus; for a while: eine Zeit lang

dressing-gown: Morgenrock

strange: merkwürdig

suspicious: Verdächtiges

shrugs her shoulders: zuckt mit den Schultern

gym: Fitnessraum

Vanessa and Marvin follow him very quietly. Suddenly Marvin kicks an exercise bicycle by accident. The man sees the children. He is shocked. He covers himself with his dressing-gown.

Plötzlich

tritt; Trimmrad; zufällig

ist schockiert; bedeckt sich

Morgenrock

"What do you want here?"

"We … er … we …", Marvin stammers.

"Get out of here!" the man says.

The children quickly leave. Outside, Vanessa says: "I know why he acts so strangely. Did you see what he did when we came in?"

Marvin remembers: "He covered himself with his dressing-gown."

"That's right. The man is ashamed because he's so fat."

"Oh, I see!" Marvin says.

Suddenly, Vanessa and Marvin feel sorry for the man. And they feel a little bit ashamed of themselves, too, because they thought he was a thief.

stammers – stottert
strangely – sonderbar
remembers – erinnert sich
covered – hüllte sich ein
dressing-gown – Morgenrock
is ashamed – schämt sich
Suddenly – Plötzlich

Mr. X

Sebastian spends every Wednesday afternoon alone at home. Today he has to copy a poem from his textbook and learn it by heart. Suddenly, the telephone rings. Sebastian answers it. At the other end of the line he hears a faint hissing sound.

"Hello?" Sebastian asks.

Nothing. Only the hissing sound.

auswendig

Plötzlich

leises Zischgeräusch

"That's strange," Sebastian says, and he replaces the receiver.

Then the phone rings again. Sebastian picks it up and gives his name. No reply at the other end.

"Hello?" Sebastian asks. "Who's there?"

Suddenly Sebastian hears a croaking voice say: "This is Mr. X. I will get you in one hour."

Sebastian drops the receiver and runs out of the flat as fast as his legs can carry him. He goes to see his friend Manuel.

Sebastian rings the bell loudly. Manuel's mother opens the door.

"What's the matter?" she asks.

"Yes, what is it?" Manuel asks.

merkwürdig
legt den Hörer auf
nimmt ab
Antwort
Plötzlich
krächzende Stimme
holen
lässt fallen
Was ist (denn) los?

"He wants to get me!" holen
"Who wants to get you?"
"Mr. X," Sebastian sniffs. schnieft
Then Sebastian tells Manuel and his mother the whole ganze story.

"I'm sure he's a naughty little boy who wants to play a trick on you," Manuel's mother says.

"We'll get *him*!" Manuel says. "Come on!" They both go into Manuel's room.

frecher
dir einen Streich spielen

holen

Manuel starts to think hard. Sebastian is still very frightened.

"This Mr. X knows that you were alone at home," Manuel says. "How did he know?"

Sebastian shrugs his shoulders.

"He must know you very well, and that you're always at home alone on Wednesdays."

"A lot of people know me," Sebastian murmurs.

"But not everyone does," Manuel says.

Sebastian agrees with him.

"During the phone call, did you hear any voices, or anything suspicious in the background?" Manuel asks.

"No voices. Only a strange hissing sound," Sebastian answers.

hat Angst

warst

zuckt mit den Schultern

murmelt

stimmt mit ihm überein

Verdächtiges

Hintergrund

seltsames Zischgeräusch

"What sort of hissing sound?"

Sebastian tries to remember. "It sounded a bit like water."

"Like water?"

Sebastian nods.

"Yes. Like a tap that won't stop running, or a flush that won't stop flushing."

Manuel thinks fast.

"Or a river?"

Sebastian thinks, then he says: "Yes, maybe."

"Then our Mr. X lives by the river," Manuel says.

"Really?" Sebastian asks.

"Of course. All we have to do is go to the river and ask who knows you there."

"But I don't know who lives there," Sebastian says. "All I know is that there's a tall building there."

Zischgeräusch
sich erinnern
ein bisschen wie
nickt
(Wasser)Hahn
zu laufen
(Klo)Spülung
zu spülen

"Sabine in our class lives by the river," Manuel says.

"But she doesn't have such a deep, croaky voice."

Only two children in the tall building are possible callers: Lukas Rogler, from Sebastian's class, and Jörg Huber from the fourth year.

Manuel and Sebastian immediately run to the tall building to solve the case.

deep, croaky voice: tief krächzende Stimme

possible callers: mögliche Anrufer

fourth year: vierte Klasse

immediately: sofort

solve; case: lösen; Fall

"Listen!" Manuel says. "We can hardly hear the water from the river here, so Mr. X's flat must be on the other side. Let's go inside and see where Jörg and Lukas live."

A woman comes out of the front door. Manuel and Sebastian slip inside behind her.

kaum

schleichen hinein

They go up the stairs and read the names on the doors. They only know that J. Huber lives at the back of the building.

"Now we've got him," Manuel says. He sees Jörg's bicycle. "Come on, why don't we let his tyres down?"

warum lassen wir ihm nicht die Luft aus den Reifen

"But what if it wasn't him?" Sebastian asks.

Aber was, wenn er es nicht war?

"It was him," Manuel says. "And even if it wasn't, we can still let the air out of his tyres because he's such a stupid show-off."

Angeber

"But we have to be sure," Sebastian says.

Then Manuel has an idea. He presses the bell marked "Huber".

Klingel; mit … gekennzeichnet

"Hello?" Jörg's voice says over the intercom.

Sprechanlage

"Come down, quickly! Someone wants to steal your bike!" Manuel says.

"I'm coming!" Jörg says.

Manuel and Sebastian hide behind the large refuse container. Jörg hurries out, sees his bike, and looks relieved.

"Hello, Mr. X!" Manuel shouts.

"Wh… what do you mean, Mr. X?" Jörg stammers. "I'm not Mr. X."

stehlen

verstecken sich

Müllcontainer

eilt hinaus

erleichtert

stottert

"Of course you are," Manuel says. "We have proof." *Beweise*

Jörg looks worried. "It wasn't me. I didn't make that phone call." *besorgt*

Manuel nudges Sebastian. "Aha, so you didn't? That's interesting. Who didn't you phone?" *stößt an*

"Nobody," Jörg says, and he runs back into the building.

"Do you believe me now?" Manuel asks Sebastian.

"What a nasty little creep!" Sebastian goes to Jörg's bicycle and lets the air out of both tyres. *gemeiner kleiner Kerl*

"The Mr. X case is closed," Manuel says. *Fall; abgeschlossen*

Dein Wörterbuch A–L

A	a bit	ein bisschen
	afterwards	danach, später
	anyway	sowieso, irgendwie, trotzdem
	at least	mindestens, wenigstens
B	back	Rücken, zurück
	bell	Klingel
	bench	(Park)Bank
	by accident	zufällig
	by heart	auswendig
C	closely	genau, streng
D	deep	tiefe
E	either … or	entweder … oder
	embarrassed	verlegen

F	flour	Mehl
	for a while	eine Zeit lang
	fridge	Kühlschrank
G	ground	Boden
H	hardly	kaum, fast nicht, nur mit Mühe
I	immediately	sofort, direkt, unmittelbar
	in advance	im Voraus
	instead	stattdessen, dafür
K	keys	Schlüssel
L	lift	Aufzug
	like	wie

Dein Wörterbuch M–T

M	mustard	Senf
N	naughty	frech, ungezogen, unartig
	neck	Hals
	noise	Geräusch, Lärm
	not … anymore	nicht mehr
O	office	Büro
	owner	Besitzer, Eigentümer
P	pepper	Pfeffer
	proudly	stolz
R	real	echt
S	sleeve	Ärmel
	slightly	ein wenig, etwas, leicht
	spoon	Löffel
	surprise	Überraschung

T	though	aber, doch, obgleich, wenn auch
	to accept	annehmen, einverstanden sein, anerkennen
	to add	hinzufügen, hinzusetzen
	to agree	einverstanden sein, einwilligen, sich einigen, vereinbaren
	to appear	erscheinen, zum Vorschein kommen, auftauchen
	to be asleep	schlafen
	to be shocked	schockiert sein, erschüttert sein
	to behave	sich benehmen
	to bet	wetten
	to blow	blasen, pfeifen, pusten, keuchen
	to cough	husten
	to cover	be-, zudecken, überziehen, einhüllen

Dein Wörterbuch T–V

T	to cross	überqueren, hinüberfahren, sich kreuzen, überschreiten
	to decide	sich entscheiden, sich entschließen
	to drop	fallen lassen
	to explain	erklären, erläutern, begründen, rechtfertigen
	to frown	die Stirn runzeln
	to grin	grinsen
	to interrupt	ins Wort fallen, unterbrechen
	to kick	treten, kicken, mit dem Fuß stoßen
	to lose	verlieren
	to mean	meinen, denken, beabsichtigen, bedeuten
	to murmur	murmeln
	to nod	nicken
	to prefer	vorziehen, bevorzugen, lieber haben, lieber tun